especially for

_____

Promises To Myself

First published in 2010 by
Red Wheel/Weiser, LLC
With offices at:
500 Third Street, Suite 230
San Francisco, CA 94107
www.redwheelweiser.com

ISBN: 978-1-57324-402-2
Library of Congress Cataloging-in-Publication Data
is available upon request.

Cover and text design by Jessica Dacher
Typeset in Agenda
Cover and interior art © Mary Anne Radmacher

Printing in Hong Kong
SS
10 9 8 7 6 5 4 3 2 1

Promises To Myself

mary anne radmacher

Conari Press

introduction

Promises: pledges we make binding ourselves to a general course, a specific action, or a commitment to someone else.

We make large and small promises daily. Refecting on the promises of my everyday deepens my satisfaction and heightens my clarity, especially in times of transition. There is a powerful intersection where a sense of purpose meets with the desire to connect. This crossing is made all the more profound in that it touches at that one point. That spot is named "Promises To Myself."

Promises begin with awareness of possibility, are affirmed by their relationship to priority and radiate outward—to return later, like homing pigeons to roost. Regardless of scope, promises begin and end within.

"I promise." Two small words with enormous impact. Every day, may you have unfettered understanding that allows you to declare, "The most important promises are the ones I make to myself."

Go ahead. Try a long look in the mirror, with the whispered words, "I promise. . ."

maryanne radmacher

Promises To Myself

the most
important
promises
are the
ones
we make to
ourselves.

In all things
and
in all ways,

may there be
wings
behind
you

(angels
ever by
you).

may
there
be
promise
before
you
(vision
drawing you
onward)

and
hope
ever
above
you
(comfort
wrapping you
in
grace).

may there be
strength
beneath
you

(enthusiam
beyond
yourself)

and in all times
and in all
experiences...
may the colors
of your soul
rise
greatly
within you
and

the light which weaves your soul to greatness

continue
to shine
and
make
a
clearer
way
for others.

our lives
are not
constructed
of well-
laid
plans or

controlled events or any other predictable thing which

may be
brewed
in the
cauldron
of our
hopes .

our lives
are simply
a succession
of
nows.

knowing this —
extend
your
hand
with the
strongest
reach

and
offer
the
best
you
are
able.

sometimes
one best
is
better
than
another.

they each
belong to
their
moment

and
added
together—

they
become
a
legacy.

one often
meets their
destiny

on
their
way

to somewhere
else.

at first glance
it may appear
too hard.

look again.
always
look
again.

walk
tall
into your day.

stand as
a
mountain.

inhabit
your body
fully.

honor
your
spirit:
listen.

embrace
your
convictions
without
apology.

whisper your
hope as
morning rain.

laugh
wildly
like
winter
thunder.

speak your
yes
firmly?

love as
deeply as
you can
reach.

fail with
grace and
enthusiasm.

overwhelm
anxiety
with
action.

create a day which will be long remembered.

the jump is so frightening between where i am and where i want to be ...

because of the
promise of
all ~ i
   may become
i will
close my
eyes and
   leap.

promises
of
friendship,
family,
and
love

may the
color that
you
brings
forth
in others rise
greatly
within you.

you
are.
wished
your
own
best
strenoth.

may
you
always
have
loved ones
by your
side,

desired
possibilities
before
you
and
contentment
behind
you.

may you know
the
beginnings
of
your dreams
and many of
the ends.

you
are
wished
peace.

listen
to the
music
of love:
in the
magnificence
of the
sea,

in the
magic
of a
child's
wonder,
in the
mischief
of any
unexpected
moment.

what joy there is
when one gets
to take
part in
the song
of
love itself

in such
promises
the open heart
and
lifted hand
, are
joined
for
good purpose.

precious child—
be blessed
in knowing
the promise
of
love
which
surrounds you.

be safe
in the
sense of
place
you
have
in your
home.

be well in
your body and
fortified
in the
growing
of
your
spirit.

may
your
strengths
and the
good
3 wishes
of your
loved
ones

guide

you

in

all

your

days.

may your sleep be protected and sweet.

May your
every day
dawn with
purpose
and
promise.

friends ————— : us.
always ————— .
travels ————————— .

stories
told and a
few kind lies.

lots
of
laughter
and
a
little
chocolate.

secrets
shared

and

tears

shed.

kindnesses
with time
in between.

dreams
and
awakenings.
long
roads.
healing
and
quiet
comforts.

wicked
mischief
and
wanton
hilarity.
time and
alway us:
friends.
always.

promises
of
possibility

this is not
about
unrealistic
planning ...
this is
reality
in
training

it is
not about
what
was.
it is
about
what
may be.

embrace
the
adventure
of the
day
while looking
forward.

dispatch tasks with ease and certainty.

lightly tap the shoulder of innovation and ask, "may i have this dance?"

imagine and move with purpose and passion.

walk

people

to

places

they never
imagined
they would
stand.

stand
with
them.

walk people
to places
they hope
to go —
but
cannot conceive
the way.

once there
stand
with
them   and
broaden their
view even
more____.

be an
excellent
vehicle —
an
inviter.

one who
draws
and entices.

one
who
coaches
from
behind and
inspires.

extend
camaraderie,
deep
humor and
shared
vision.

march
in a parade
that shall

always

be

remembered

as you.

promises
to the
world

the call to
serve
takes
many
forms
in the life
of a
compassionate
heart.

in the
reach to
assist,
inadvertently
we
lift
ourselves

dance is the way the body spells

we tell the
tale of our
life
by the
stories
we repeat
each day.

walking
your
promise
makes
every
journey
a road of
joy.

what is a
voice if it
does not
raise
against
injustice?

what is a
voice
if it does not
sing
for
change
or
speak for
the
silent?

what
is a
voice

if it merely
mimics
the
machinations
of our culture?

a still
voice is a
dried reed,
lost
toy.

torn
page...

a
broken
feather
floating
down
an
emptied
canyon.

what is a
voice if it
remains
silent
against
leagues of
tyranny?

it is the
tremble
of risk
that
shakes the
spirit.

confirms courage, and reinstates promise.

to our readers

Conari Press, an imprint of Red Wheel/Weiser, publishes books on topics ranging from spirituality, personal growth, and relationships to women's issues, parenting, and social issues. Our mission is to publish quality books that will make a difference in people's lives—how we feel about ourselves and how we relate to one another. We value integrity, compassion, and receptivity, both in the books we publish and in the way we do business.

Our readers are our most important resource, and we value your input, suggestions, and ideas about what you would like to see published. Please feel free to contact us, to request our latest book catalog, or to be added to our mailing list.

Conari Press
An imprint of Red Wheel/Weiser, LLC
500 Third Street, Suite 230
San Francisco, CA 94107
www.redwheelweiser.com